Searching the Drowned Man

Searching the Drowned Man

Poems by Sydney Lea

University of Illinois Press
Urbana Chicago London

Library of Congress Cataloging In Publication Data

Lea, Sydney, 1942–
  Searching the drowned man.

  I. Title.
PS3562.E16S4   811'.5'4   79–26565
ISBN 0–252–00796–4
ISBN 0–252–00798–0 pbk.

Acknowledgments

The author would like to thank the editors
of the following magazines for permission to
reprint certain poems in this volume:
"Searching the Drowned Man," *Ascent;* "To
the Summer Sweethearts," "To Our Son,"
"For Don C., against a Proverb," "Recalling
the Horseman Billy Farrell from an Airplane in
Vermont," *Hudson Review;* "Vermont: August
Fever," *Virginia Quarterly Review;* "Night Patrol:
The Ancestral House," *Poetry Northwest;*
"Duck Hunter," "Elegy at Peter Dana Point,"
"Night Message for Ted in the South," "The
Urge to Appropriate," *Southern Review;*
"Revision of the Seasons," *Salmagundi;* "Her
Watches: In a Dry Time," "Drooge's Barn,"
"Father's Game," *Sewanee Review;* "Band
Concert," *Beloit Poetry Journal;* "Young Man
Leaving Home," *Prairie Schooner;* "The
President of Flowers," "Regarding the Figures in
Children's Wisdom," "Night Trip across the
Chesapeake and After," "For My Son Creston
at the Solstice," *Texas Review;* "A Dream near
Water," *Massachusetts Review;* "Searches for a
Friend," *Quarterly West.*

  "The Train Out" originally appeared in *The
New Yorker.*

For Richard Selzer: model, friend

Now is now, and then was then, and Yule's in winter.

Contents

Searching the Drowned Man: The Third Day

"—I don't like the idea of what we're going to find."
—Bill White, search boss

After the two days of oiled calm
that morning the wind
blew up, ranging Grand Lake in lines
of foam.   Depending
on how you felt about the idea,
dread or hope
picked up as well. He'd be on the eastern
shore, where pines
bowed inland in November's gale from north-
northwest.   At last
we'd find him in the gut by Kolekill Island,
bobbing on cobby
beachstones, bright in autumn sun
as a different prospect.
But in that small canoe, incon-
sequential splash
of green like an afterthought on the blue-
near-black of the lake,
I called up other images:
                                    the whited
eye of the broke-kneed
timber horse that drifted against
the dam in town
in August, minnows schooled in the putrid
cave of stomach.
The bloated belly-up suckers that clogged
The Wabass culvert

after the logging crew blew up
that beaver flowage.
The nauseating stink of the mill
when the breeze comes south.
How few, I thought, can swim! I was
the lone exception,
I who had joined the search in my young
man's search of ideas.
My father, an uncle and aunt, a boyhood
friend had died
behind some curtains.
                              A raft of hooded
mergansers fell in
downwind of our ragged hunting flotilla,
the slightest of lees.
A fish-hawk screamed just once above
and shot the blow
out of sight over Farm Cove Mountain, whose bald
top winnowed clouds
like chaff as they galloped past. My knuckles
ached on the paddle.
I strained to store these signals up.
One day they'd be
the recollected lineaments
of what I'd found,
what felt.   And what
could I have been expecting, the Angel
Death? On finding
the man, the canoes to eddy like leaves
and blow off the map?
                              Did I hunt some grim articulation

from grinning lips
of the victim (who after all was only
the halfwit Lowery
from Springfield whom I half-knew, who never
had any luck)?
Whatever I'd thought,
it wasn't this
declarativeness, a face that looked
engaged by plainest ideas: Now where
did I leave my jacket,
shoes? Hands raised up as if
to ward off gnats.
The body whole in its nondescript suit
of fishing clothes.
Flesh unrent by imagined turtles
who sink into boredom
as winter peeks through the fall, though clouds
and lake and mountain
and wind go on
as they have gone without repose.

Premises

The Tracks on Kenyon Hill

You struggle out. Wet with the South,
the snow that blew all night has roused you
from a dream of filth to a dream of filth.
The windowpanes are smeared. The brush
and trees are coated as with bird lime.
Weather's hung itself like phlegm
on reappearing berry vines
as drifts sink down to spring.

At dawn you mopped your cabin floor,
turned up the weak-kneed chairs on the table,
the way you've seen them do—a stranger
woman on your arm, gin keening
in the close-packed folds of either ear—
in city stores at midnight.
You've laughed at this impermanence
surrounded by impermanence.

Laughed . . . the way these rooms seem set
to vanish upward through their roofs.
The snow persists, a big wet brush.
Can you track yourself back? And why
have you chosen solitude so long?
Your tracks become a smear against the hill.
You know. That's what there is to know,
unlike the prints you come upon
to northward of the stone fence: large
but somehow dainty. They seem to have
three toes, when you can make them out.
You'll follow. But you dally
at a place where limbs have sagged across

a gully, for this thing has shouldered
slush from off the boughs, head-high.

In your head the cabin gleams, so clean,
transparent now, it seems to rise
upward from muddy ground. You drop
down to your knees, and still the track
—the closer that you look—looks back
at you, more distant, the way a word
will do: *self; plan; object.*
You recall an ancient tribe that figured

life as a gigantic bird,
three-toed. Confused, you rise.
The hemlocks puff a mist like tarsmoke.
To you the woods have never seemed
so dark and dirty. It's the season's
gray cloacal jumble. Gray
of March, the runoff. Back of you,
your tracks have turned into a swirl.
Ahead, a shape gets up and gets away.

Young Man Leaving Home

Over the dropped eggs and hash, his elders
poured unaccustomed benedictions.

The morning broke fair, but they
insisted on sensing rain.

That last spring, after so many,
the tree with the rope swing blossomed,

random plum blooms dropping groundward
where the playhouse leaned.

Later, the tracks with their switchbacks among
the shanties outside the station

had a somewhat surprising Protestant look
of a hopeless proposition.

Adieu: to the father who fobbed and fondled
his watch, at the end of his chain,

whose simple grief no halting final
declaration seemed to soften;

to the mother feigning impatience
with the lateness of the train.

They. Tree. House. Yard.
All had called for his valediction,

but now was already the hour prior
to greeting whatever it is that this is,

hour of assembly, of public instead
of certain longed-for private kisses,

hour of livered grandmothers, aunts,
whose cheeks the plain tears stained. . . .

It passed in the fashion of dreams, at once
chaotic and sluggish.

En route: in silence, he hailed The Future,
that unimaginable lode of riches,

this hero, composed of a dozen young rebels
out of thin novels, groaning with luggage.

To the Summer Sweethearts

The easiness of August night:
a fall of meteors,
moths jewel my house

across the lane, I float
in the fire-pond, in the light-
riffled fire-pond. Cattails puff
their buoyant seed. The tadpoles
have absorbed their tails:
they hum and pause and hum.

Innocent, I ask you in.

The egg-rich mayflies dip and rise,
dimple the surface, die.
The silver guppies sip them.

Come sit, at least, composite
(eyes of Margot, Susie's hair,
the even smile of Sarah),
there on the bank.
You've seen the evil-looking turtles,
but sweetheart they never bite.

There. There.
Let's have a look at you.

Listen to the Whip-Poor-Will,
Chuck-Will's-Widow,
Nightjar.

Father's Game

for David Huddle

Blue as birds' eggs, smoke
from his cigar sank in-
to gentle summer air,
cooling after supper.
Yellowjackets whizzed
like shot among the sugar
cubes and peach pits. This
was how we played the game:
a point for every dog
that he could whistle in.
Eight is the best I remember:
a glum-eyed basset, tandem
stiff-legged poodles from
a block downstreet where William
Gold played "My Blue Heaven"
night after night on his
piano, trebles winging
through the sycamores,
four fruitcake mutts, and even
a strange basenji which,
because it never came
again, we nicknamed "Prophet,"
a joke my little sisters
missed, despite his patient
explanation. "Prophet"
became a laughing word
whenever heard, for me
and for my brothers; even
my religious mother smiled

her own sad smile. That siren
whistle was a signal
he'd perfected, waiting
somewhere in Wales for D-Day.
John Whitney, town and army
chum, had turned his head
to hear it just before
the bullet jolted in
behind his ear near Dieppe.
Miles and years away,
sometimes a stray that sidles
down our road recalls
the smoke-and-coffee smell
of lazy evenings and
my father, whistling in the dark.

Her Watches: In a Dry Time

Doubt burns at her
like sun of these days.
Midnight, falling
out of sleep and in:
she dreams herself
an old blind thing,
runs her hands
across a ridge of Braille; the child,
because he's not a book,
begins to squall.
He will not have her kneading.

•

A rooster blurts his own mistake
for dawn. Her breasts hang numb,
her past is crinkling
like a map, blue scrawls
of water, vein,
turn like old ink to brown.

•

Town bells clap
red dust to settle
on the steeple swallows.
Ducks, for want of water, flee
over Moody Mountain,
bruised in the drought.
The hens have sucked
the eggs she planned for breakfast.

•

A crowd of ocher pigeons moans
and rattles in the mow.
The day moon is a cuticle,
the hay broadcasts a sorry stink
at noon, the bull snuffs in his shed;
her man is soldered to his scythe.
What words does she have?

•

Evening meal: the squirrels
rustle in the crackling eaves-troughs,
voices grown ridiculous, thin.

•

Because the brooks are gone, at night
a train of eels goes overland
in dew. They gum the fallen
squash vines. Eleven withered stars
appear, and field rats gnaw
the roots of river weed.

•

The child gropes for her
reservoirs: paps, marrow, moisture of her eyes.

Night Message for Ted in the South

Neat as a knife, last night's storm tore
in two the tree that marks this trail.
That moony glim in the trunk's dust core
is foxfire, the light—they say—in hell.

Your ma wouldn't talk to your papa. He,
a preacher unfrocked for some philander,
raised prize white goats for the fairs, and she
raised roses. Somehow, the goats would wander

out of their pens to eat the flowers.
For which she shot them. You got a taste
for walks at dark. Clocks slouched the hours,
groaned arpeggios. Your parents paced

in separate rooms, black housemaids yawned
a final time, and heaved downhill to bed.
A hound, far off, would bawl the swamp;
the junebugs cracked against you, you said,

and in the pine-straw, rodents chittered.
Later, you joked at what neighbors called
"those folks on the hill." But an older sister
stayed there and died. The sheriff hauled

your broken brother, wild drunk, to prison.
Gone north, you hiked now in lead-filled air
among the pigeons. I'd come to listen
to the family farce, or else to hear

you dream out loud of your rambling nights.
At dark, we sat where bluesmen blew
their down-home runs under muted lights.
The shimmering horns reminded you,

you'd tell me, of the foxfire.
In the end, you moved back south, and I
went the other way: up here.
Still, in your letters, you would say

(before they stopped) how the very ground
you walked at sundown refused to alter,
how blooming in nightlight you sometimes found
a rusted cartridge or a goat's rotted halter.

Here, a broken tree gaps pale.
Signs must tell us where we are,
or nothing. All the brooks are full
of the cleft moon cruising down the stars.

A Dream near Water

for John Engels

You walk toward the river. White flecks in your beard have
    gone;
But so has the beard.   Completely.   You're surprised,
Bending to cup up water, at the glossy tone

Of your skin. You notice too the wave and swell
Of your arms.   All the women — girls, really —
You have ever known: they seem to be wishing you well

From the opposite leafy bank. As one, they stand
In smiles, wearing the billowy loose beach suits
Of another time, breeze-ruffled, extending their hands.

It's before the invention of clocks, or any chronometer.
(Amazing, what this means to time in the dream.)
So save your distinctions — *happy, sad* — for later.

For you feel no desire. You'll recall a pleasant view
And directly, the taste of water so clean you'll ache,
But not until awake, with something like sorrow.

Slim birds are fluting from the clickety reeds,
Pastels. Your children aren't a factor. Summer
Looms, as wide as ocean.   This soft morning haze

Will be half the day burning off, uncountable hours
Will pass before your father sends up to your window,
Through which the dusk air puffs a scent of flowers,

His familiar whistle of greeting.   He's come home
From a day trip on the lake. Later, he'll mount
The stairs to tuck you away in the violet room

Where, for a time that passes slow as an age,
You attend to tales that provoke unthinking laughter,
To your mother whose sobs are beading like dew on the page,

To the June frogs that wake and call to you over calm water.

Vermont: *August Fever*

Blue deepens, sucks
the children's shouts away
as crickets creep
to the ballfield, trill and scrape.
His radio whispers
from another time zone:
the Plains states beg
for rain, have even called
—out of his room
in a county "home"—
a Kiowa shaman to drool
his invocation, shaking bones.

Here, a distant
lightning caps bamboo
(persistent shoots
he has fought each spring to kill)
with pearled light.
His old dog drags her haunches
under the bed.
The idiot insects clap
for entry at the screen.
A moth does hara-kiri
on the book of gloomy
stories he handles.   A wash of dust
falls on the page.
The inner throb of fever
claims the rhythm
of the all-but-vanished peepers.

A cough in the quiet . . .
and how the blue has drenched him!
He follows the course
in mind of a boyhood ball
—free at last—
that climbed into the blue.
The radio gutters
like a candle.   So much has flown.

Bells boom
their final time at nine.
He dreams his bones
have blued, and whisper something
in atavistic syllables. The first
fat drops tink counter-
point upon the tin.
In dream, a boy
comes on the lawn to stand
and look up to
the skies.   Now he sinks in

to sleep, his summer sickness,
blue, a kind of peace.

To Our Son

"Take care. A child's world is full of pretty poisons."
  —brochure from the Poison Control Center

Child, take heed
of iodine, bright
as your fire truck shining,
of flame, of poinsettia,
of bronze rhubarb leaves,

of pills like baubles,
tranquilizers,
candy-sheathed killers
of pain, and emerald
tabs for an early sleep.

You've come home dazzled
with tears, with news
"so bad I want it
out of my mouth."
A friend, "the nicest

girl in class,"
has died. So much
to keep from your reach:
the pretty poisons,
then absences—

the aunt who moved
to Finland, a doll,
a road-killed bird,

the nicest girl. . . .
Careful, we grasp

the center's message,
read indications
in your pains: in scratches
on skin; in subtle
indigos, purples,

hennas and browns
that ring your bruises;
in scarlet maps
grown out of infection;
and now your urge

to spit out meaning,
and all the little
wounds, and large.

The President of Flowers

His wife referred to him as "Honey-Dripper,"
and it's true, in memory there is a sweet
association—sugared talk and whiff
of Sweet William, citric tang of the compost heap
in which his soft black hand threw everything,
even jars and bottles, for "glass ain't a thing
but sand blowed up, and sand it's bound to be
again one day." By which he must have meant,
though I was full of adolescent rage
and couldn't know it then, that death
was a thing too individual to count
for much among so many grander patterns.
                                              I only
sought to tell the old man truth: "Great God!
The black man in this land has no damned power!"
He warned me not to curse, then laughed like wind
along my parents' cherry orchard, nights:
"Son, I am the President of Flowers."
Poppies showed him, as they showed to no one else,
their bashful tongues. I swore that apples hung
in clusters before their blossoms fell away.
Exotic currants swelled our silver platter.
He grew a Pennsylvania avocado,
the only one I've ever seen, or heard of.
And then, toward fall, that strangest bloom—his cancer.

But he bent with it as he was used to bending,
and grapes came on more purple than before.
He gave up water, told me how the pain
would die of drought. He drove his truck to Georgia,
a visit to the family. There, he dug
a payload full of Dixie loam because

our Iris bed was full of bugs with claws.
"That red will quick-walk those old rascals down."
And *something* made them go. His death was like him,
slow: in alien odors of his darkened
house I sensed him—temples falling in,
a boyish skin, hands kneading at the folds—
and inhaled the jab of ruined marigolds.

In mem. Alex Lewis

For My Father, Who Hunted

> . . . great as is the pleasure of becoming acquainted with the stars and
> planets, greater still the joy of recognizing them as friends, returning after
> absence. . . .
>
> —*A Beginner's Star Book*

A late beginner, I was struggling with
an early chapter: "Learning to Observe."
I have no faith in stars, in omens—nothing
there prepared me for the uncle's phone call

or the nothings sent back from the hospital,
laid out: a watch, a dollar nine in coin;
yet I hold, despite disastrous evidence,
a faith in language: *planet,* say,

from dim old names for *wanderer.* It has no place
that's certain like the stars'. Come near,
it kindles in the sky; or, wandered off,
it loses glory: that I've learned

is "occultation." Now all detail shines,
with a trace of brightness recognized,
though words obscure: the pheasant's fire
of feather in the dark of afternoon;

river waves rebounding noon's white slap;
the pickerelweed at false dawn flickered orange
above my spread of decoys.   All
have, in your absence, influence; and down,

as if to swing a leg across our log fence,
climbs Orion.   Or minutiae
rise up in mind and air: your wallet
spilling silver and your watch

in constellation, sweep hand sweeping back
the seconds, minutes fallen down.

Night Patrol: The Ancestral House

for A. B. Paulson

As he shakes it out,
his uncle's pup tent
exhales a cloud of moths, his army
outfit—at ease in a corner—
glows in a slick of camphor.

His generations sleep.
He steals
to each extreme: top floor and basement
and storage closet, clothes hung there like thieves.
Brocade on the shelves

handed from daughter
to daughter to daughter;
in a wicker case, a wedding photo
of elders unknown: the man's look is hard;
in the background a bugler, a color guard.

The return is a silence
broken only
by the lurch of a water pump, unsteady
as parents' snoring, the boiler's hum.
A small boy's drum

detects his parade
on the stairs—its springs
shift and whisper like weeds. The costumes . . .
some power that he would put on.

Here, a prayer book bound in silver
pulses in darkness like a clot of phosphor.

There, the navy
airplane he never
finished assembling, that Christmas dawn,
because of some battle with his dead father
that his dead mother thought was beneath her.

His generations
breathe at the ends
of old corridors. At attention,
he stands;
the regimented hours shrink
close, close around him, then break rank.

The Train Out

Fluff from his lap robe hangs in a rift
in the curtains, as his eyes un-gum.
Nebraska yawns. Mergansers shift
in their mudholes. Morning: aluminum
track sheds begin to flare.

Blood ticks in his temples. Where
did he toss his coat, his keys?
As well in Topeka. Inanities
from a dream of her linger—a china jug,
hot liquor, a room

he cannot place. A tinsel bug
revives against the kindling panes.
Stiff old porters in the corridor
swear to a time when "a train was a train,"
mutter against the diesel's roar.

A green dead dawn. . . .
All borders are ends. . . .
He conjures a cove; a bed; a song;
rings and a necklace; a barbered lawn.

A catalogue past. Old words, thick as wax.
Exhaust expires in a feint of wind,
and the sun glows dull on the tracks.

Early Snow.   Demmick Hill Site.   Full Moon.
One Man

for Don Metz

The eyes of his children's
jack-o'-lantern: filled with October
snow.   And how, this one man asks,
can this ever be peace? The cornstalks shiver,
nodding together, whisperers fanning
mean imaginings.
Forenoon stretches long
as an idea of winter.
He chooses the moon
for cure. The weather
in oddest sympathy clears
by two in the afternoon.

All nature—groundswell,
blowdown, scarp—appears
to lean against his climb
eastward, up the steepest ridge.
Clutching at breakable root and limb,
he arrives at length at land's height,
sweeps a circle of woodsfloor clean,
rigs his tent tight,
gathers wisps of tinder, ever-
green boughs and branches for cooking.
He wants to believe
it's only a matter of looking. . . .
How easy, tonight,
if it were so:

woodsfloor, ridge and mountain,
draw, hill, hollow,
even each pine-spill and leaf
are self-conscious with light.
New snow like old remorse
holds to ground, to trees,
illumined. The moon's strict gaze
betrays each flaring rodent pursued
by soft-padded chaser or winged one,
each flaring, also betrayed
by light.   One odd man in the night
sits still as rock
and feels his labor,
his will to construct
a self. Assured.
Aloft. Aloof
above the far town's chimneys,
square yards, amortized roofs.
But cold is nibbling at his bootsoles,
as if with a will to bore
into his mind in reflection,
into his flesh's core.
The hand that fans his embers,
the teeth he picks as free
as he can of gobbets and cinders,
even the funneled stomach sucking
his rough food down—
all seem to gleam,
illumined, more real than they've been
and more unknown.
There is something. . . .

High in its arc, the moon:
a reckless explosive pumpkin.
In spite of this
unusual brightness it's late
to think of escape,
and home's not simply too tangled and far,
but full of as many accumulations,
double meanings, strange laws and mirrors.

A chilly, anachronistic
frog is calling him to a springhole
like someone else's unsettled soul.
He steps in caution there.
His eyes, reflected in midnight water,
fill with the cold light's stare.
He shudders,
returns, lays on a bough,
resolved, resolved
to close the eyes now
though the earth of his site
won't warm to one man's fire,
and moon inclines ever more
to frankness, not desire.

Revisions

Incantation against Revelation

On that day there shall be neither cold nor frost. And there shall be continuous day (it is known to the Lord), not day and not night, for at evening time there shall be light.

—*Zechariah* 14:6

Let it not be.
Let winter-clipped day
rush to dark
and insufficient clarity
of partial light from impartial moons.
All day,
let snow drift over
famished vision,
slat fences be buried
like bones in our meat
or an instinct, hidden
in harmless
indecipherable charades of sleep.
In darkness.
Let Lord not be one Lord, not be
Lord of One.

Let the country have night
in which beasts
predictably fool us
with their footfalls, cries
spilling from mazy
buckbrush, trees.
None like another.
Let the country be
full of animal rites:

the nightjar's click and hum in praise
of his mate, the fox's
imperfect circle
round his bed before bedding.
Woodcock tumble
through skies of April.
All day, a mystery of bees.

Let prophecy of the day the fall
foliage will turn
remain inept,
and evergreen tamaracks
turn to ferns,
their cascades of yellow needles a sign,
and nothing to signify.
Let cold and frost descend
to freeze the slap
of a million waves
in difficult runes over hosts of fry
of cloudiest fate. Let people not cry
the one tear designed
to end tears.
Let many a woman and man
for the cloudiest reasons be brave.

And let there be years,
seasons, the colorful comings
and goings of grief,
bolting flowers, exquisite
unmeaning in all
our protests at darkness,
pleas for relief.

Let an ending to number
be unimaginable:
butterflies
—vulnerable Monarchs—dismay
with their profligate stratagems,
wind-battered waste-motion miles;
in suicide
barnacles cluster
like salt clots over the piles

of docks, as many as seeds
of mustard, in harbors of cities
bigger than Zion
where the harsh bouquet of sulfur
clouds and softens
the looming high-rises like pity
so that out of discomfort
rises high splendor
and nowhere is pure
white Light
nor reduction in mind's quantity. . . .
Let us suffer. . . .
Let us hail
the intimate hum of insects, say,
returning by thousands at night

and say
at least at last, There is
this order prevails.

Regarding the Figures in Children's Wisdom

for Donald Justice

Look. The evening star.
Now in old books
herdsmen drive bleating
flocks to the fold.
This composition
might resemble peace,
but the children regard
the elders' shadows
on walls, hard hands
on lamb-white sheets.

A smell of whiskey.
A far suffering dog.
Twilit swallows
transform themselves
in their regard.
Outside, the park
fills with sublimer
patterns of bat
and dream, familiar.
Streetlamps ignite.

For some, the evening
is nostalgia—lost love,
jonquils bobbing
with simile:
butter; tarnished
gold; memory.

The children's figures
are fiercer: heat
in the eyes of looming
fathers; foxfire;

meteors; nightclocks' glow. . . .
On the pavement, a man
in a black lamb coat
regards the shadows
move on the walls,
safe in his semblance
of melancholy.
What was that thing he read in school?
Something or other . . .
La crépuscule. . . .

Pastels, perfumes. . . .

The Urge to Appropriate

"... those who desire to be rich fall into a temptation, a snare. ..."
— 1 Timothy 6:10

The western ridge grows rose
along its rim;
new clouds of April settle,
as the evening cools,
like petals.

No prudent man would set a trap
if, as he did, his quarry sat
upstream to watch him
check the toggle, cock the tine,
as if arranging flowers.

But false spring baits you
with her nubs of grass,
wet mist, white sun
as round as any dollar.
She spreads herself before you,

like bouquets or jewels,
opens her arms and breathes,
"Here I am again."
And again,
you grasp at her like silver.

After the sodden-leather winter
you get greedy.
Sudden change brings out in you

the acquisitor:
you'd possess each plant and beast,

though tonight the dew gems into glass,
the cold comes down and they escape you.
You draw on your self-pity.
Bankrupt, snared, you have the nerve to be

exorbitant—to think of great spring martyrs,
thinking they are your brothers,
though it's with envy you consider
the lilies of the field.
You're broke, but dream you can afford

to speculate, though it's down, down deep,
that buds uncurl, and far away that mink sluice through
rich cress in early eddies. And the beaver sleep,
denned up amid their hoards.

Night Trip across the Chesapeake and After

for Stanley and Hope Plumly

Mind a clutter: sick with love for another
woman, and set on murder (wildfowl would dive
next day to our brush-built blind). The diesel smeared
air with its fumes. Its wake roiled clumps of phosphor.
The hunters' "paradise" was a spit of land to the north
of Tangier Island. Dragged up from a barge, tin trailers
shuddered to windward amid knife-thin headstones
with jackets of slime. The marsh to the south was rank
with ages of feather-strewn nests and tangled lines
for crab, fish, otter. It weltered in weather,
sighing resignation.   The cooking station
reeked coal oil and antimacassars drenched
in sweat and the cheap pomade of insular men
and women. One saw one's life. A clotted flock
of newsy letters, cozy ancestral bones
that leaned from too many mantelpieces, squalid
crowd to be joined, babies' playthings, spattered
food, old grease in a covey of rusted spiders.

Come dawn, they swarmed: inedible shags and scoters.
They croaked black warning against desire.
Barnacles crept observably over the wharf-posts,
thickened with ruin. The rain was steady, soaking.
Thoughts were kin to the wrack of lowest tide.
The mudflats smelled, o God, like hell.   The front
came suddenly on, from an antithetical quarter:
a cobalt-colored sky advanced against
the obvious wind. The boats of oyster dredgers
weighed their anchors, scudding free as stallions.

"Don't know what's in that rim," said Don our guide,
a different hue in his eyes. Rafts of coots
and trash-ducks rose, headed for weedy bayou,
moss-choked brake.   Only the trumpeting hosts
of swans flew pure and wonderful into the weather.
Don the guide spat his cud of Red Man away,
declaring, "I'd just as soon shoot down an angel."
A cold breath swept the bay.

Constellation

"The baby woke up. I've gone to buy yogurt."
                    —memo from my wife

Awake, I hobble to this odd connection scrawled
on a postcard showing Millet's twilit Reaper.
But I am keen to all the odd connections:
foremost, how I am shelter and support
to me, in process of decay and fracture,
how I sweated in the icy air to keep myself
in shape—sweated, fell, and broke an ankle;
how it throbs in its stiff chamber like a brain.

Gray matter. The house grows dusky, but in pity
of myself, I do not struggle to a light.
March hail melts into nothing on a sill
outside. Pain makes the only stars I'll see.
Archaic poets punned on all they sought
in sex's ecstasy. They called it Death.
How far inferior, the mystery
that links an infant girl to soured curds.

The silence, as an old saw has it, deafens—
till child and woman enter, puffing fog.
They sunder meditation, and the clouds
—as if on cue from metaphors outworn—
wheel up, revealing Love's old constellation:
moonlight casts my plaster cast in silver,
turns the mother's hair to ghostly silk,
shines along the baby's rainbow visage,

lustrous in its film of berry, milk.

43

Searches for a Friend

Red Hollow: a stillness

Midday.   You ride into it.   Lifeless.   Even insects
hide, in the musty shine of tree holes,
or set themselves on trunk or bough: still
as small gnurls.   Your horse's belly,
from hay that smelled like fish,
grates like a strap hinge.

The day's recesses gape.
In the hollow, your mind angles shallow
noon for words: your vanished friend
once felt this flatness, heat; and still
you want to follow,
though his tracks are gone.   In talc-like dirt,

the horse drools, snuffles, raising
a mist of dust to gag you.
Years here were nothing, he might have said,
had you found him: only hatred for the standstill
that a farm is—beasts of little instinct, barn pests,
comings-on of crops, each seedling

an iteration, the same, the same:
those rows and rows of green.
So he fled, or died. You do not know.
Over you, fixed to its string of breath,
an airplane fades into abstract blue. . . .

44

You check yourself, for you
begin to make analogy, and want,
at any cost, conclusion.
Spur him up. Move on.

The Train Yard

The horse died under you. You walked away.
One of his nostrils rounded like a mouth.
His legs showed botfly eggs. Gnats circled
the eyes, gummed green. You walked, you thought,
away; but the carcass swells before you.

The rail tramps scratch at their oval frypans.
One loco one treads an ellipse. He chants,
"O!" West of you, the sun suffuses
globes on stilts: the water towers. Balls of smoke
float up from idling trains and hobo fires.

To search the friend turns you back mute
on yourself. You hunker in the ring of stiffs
who hand stale spirits round a flaming barrel.
In a dream he rides, in an engine, past
your hailing, through the darkened roundhouse.

A Ridge near Home

You pass your neighbor, eyes down. November, month
of provender. He leaves off hilling bulbs
to watch you. Childlike, you crack the puddle ice.
It shoots quick veins like mica.

The recollections: wide boyhood orchards,
a bike, a fish, your father's hound
of the hazy voice. It is a choice
to love or mean to love this season,
its aftermaths: the sun redoing
a rusted roof, crystals in cowdung,
tawny sidehills, rudeness of crows
in bleak dark trees.

Yet this place and time
of year—you'll find
no friend here, though familiar rock
and runnel mark your progress up.
There, you saw an ermine flick away one March.
And here, a sleet storm bent the beeches:
too many paid, but how they glittered! gorgeous,
like blood on barbed wire. Beside the brook,
pale scats quilled with hair:
the bobcat's gone, in search of surer ground.
What small romance the ridge once had
is gone as well. But then some smell

blows off a ruined hayfield; flights
of grosbeaks burst from stunted hemlock,
thick as insects. Far away, a lovesick bull
drools and blares dissatisfaction. Balls of smoke
on Township Mountain, where they've hung so many
seasons. Your friends, your family
have been here—they're still, or gone
in smoke of train or plane. What have you?

Circles, fading, weak simile. You see
your neighbor right himself as you walk down—
finished with planting, old back bowed from work.
Resolve: You will treat him like a brother,

hail him, speak his name. It is your own.

Duck Hunter

for Stephen Arkin

Sleet drives at his jaw like a dentist's tool.
His hands are clubs, the weather sideways,
gray the water, eelweed, air.

Nothing scales from the sky.

He'd smoke, but his matches spread red pulp
like goo the beaten boxer gloves away.
Ice like coarse shot clicks in his hair.

What are these strivings, mornings,
for a fugitive control?

> He hears the freight from Canada,
> its whistle soft but the echo a bellow.
> It is keeping time.

> Before the blow, he groped for his boat
> and flushed a belated nightjar: wings
> popped like a luffing sail.

> He could not place the pounding beavers
> or the absent streak of moon above
> the slough; but, choiceless, they are his.

Upriver people snuff and snore in houses black as dens.
On the wind his thoughts cross to them,
flap under sill and sash and come back.

They dream on.

He quickens, he'll believe,
in a kind of cold adversity.

He will be late again for work,
mumbling excuses, full of meaning,

his mind elsewhere.

For My Son Creston at the Solstice

I've made a life.   Walking these ridges at dawn,
even in winter, when it seems no dawn will come:
pitiable minutes of daylight front the dark,
the wild things' tracks become so frozen-rimmed
my dogs ignore them.   Late into morning, owls
still whiffle past.   I tell myself that we
are December children, Creston.   We ought to know
births, beginnings out of the least suggestion.
In your high-built bed you're dreaming now, I'll guess,
of comic-book heroes facing almighty space.
They never fail.   The snow's untimely deep,
so I follow my own old trail: to ramble off
today would be to fall to the throbbing knees,
reminders of old injury, the treacherous
crust would chip at my blood.   Walking these ridges,
I tell myself I've made a kind of life.

Now sleep.   In time you'll learn the signs I have
by heart.   A small bird's track.   See how he steps
and stops and pecks.   You'll notice how one toe
is missing at the knuckle, his print a compass rose
without an East.   Here he flutters (wing tips
brushing the dust), lands and cocks his head.
I'd almost said this silly ball of fluff
and I were of one mind. True, if at all,
by half or less. His mind is not on love.
He sensed that there was danger from on high
(that's why he skipped), but didn't wonder what
it was. An ice storm's beaten down the hemlock
here. I see the house. The fluming chimneys,
snow dams on the eaves. Breathing hard, I whisper

"I've made a life," dream your mother risen,
your sister gazing at the mystery of her toes,

your morning clear before you as a pasture
after blizzard. Circling west, I drop
down to last August's campsite, where we cooked
and sang. So help me God, you'll never know
how long—while summer's light kept hovering over
Stonehouse Mountain—I sat before the tent flap,
far more crazy than I'd ever been, a sentry
warding off vague phantoms.   The slow-winged dark
filled with boding nightbirds, more single-minded
than I was or am. You were uncanny white
as snow. The canvas caught up the pathetic
sweetness of your breath.   I wept, the way a phony
hero does, exposed.   By now you're clothed.
Look.   The hares have shambled through our fireplace
on their run.   I'll tear away the hardpack.   There!
Old coals are flaring in the fierce new sun.

The Bus to Schenectady

The Greyhound groans along the freeway. Nerves
cannot compose in the whizz of chromed projectiles,
eighteen-wheelers. There, a wrecker hauls
a metal nightmare from the tricky shoulder; cruisers
flicker blue; an orange ambulance
shrieks east and down a ramp. What old lament
is apt? How trivial is this traveler,
concerned for song! The weather—March and Mud—
remains mere weather, although he wants to hang
the strains of long-gone music in its grime and hail.
But Elegy! It is you who die, who fail.

The engine hums below. The weary traveler
has become all eye and ear, aghast at these
who gobble snacks and moot their politics,
who say—and seem unmoved to say—"The world
has gone to hell," and praise this or the other
jukebox cowboy ("Can't that old boy cry?"),
who curse the slush and faltering hockey teams—
for who among them can he ever dream in sad
procession, mourning what they never knew
had lived? That fellow reading in the aisle?
The Sunday funnies make him smile.

The mourners must come winging out of books
if they're to come at all. Yet Theocritus,
Moschus, Spenser, his belovèd Milton
all are dead. All dead. The gnashing gears,
the whining tires can roll them back to hell
and pave it over. And why think more of flowers?
The bus is sliding past a foam-choked river:

he cannot deck the tomb with condoms, cans,
the nameless floating brush in spring's brown thaw.
Best summon some nostalgic, bitter don
to heap his paper garlands on.

At last Schenectady. Is this synechdoche?
Our knowing traveler believes he reads a world
in knots of mooching derelicts, in tumbling bricks,
beyond the reach of any elegy.
If anything, the cops make it cohere.
The traveler finds himself the bitter don;
he snaps his briefcase shut and hails a cab,
ignores the driver's voluble small-talk,
shuts his eye and ear to hopeless din
that echoes in the dust-and-asphalt lots.
He has had enough of vacant lots.

In an orange-and-white motel he snores in fits
and sweats awake. The radiators steam.
In dreams, dead masters rise into the sky.
He gaps and heaves a window open, breathes
the fetid mist that blows in from the Hudson.
The quick strobe lights of cruisers, twisted wrecks
of truck and auto, keening ambulance,
the chitchat in the bus, a tragic cowboy's tune,
Sunday funnies, grating gears, loud tires—
these all compose themselves, as in a miracle.
The traveler grows lyrical:

above the city's sulphur-laden reek
a morning star pokes out. He thinks he sees
at last what he's resisted seeing, thinks

he hears in gabble of the bus and sooty town
the measure of a life, as if epiphany
were nothing more than fact. His thoughts come down
to this: No god in nature but as if in nature,
not to him revealed in full for now.
He knows his file of ancient mourners, though,
have passed into their darkness; yet the dark
outside the window isn't dark

because the modes he's known and loved are gone.
He pads into the motel's plastic shower
(walls and curtains covered all in flowers).
Old cadences explode in his new song.

for Peter Travis, who understood . . .

Recalling the Horseman Billy Farrell
from an Airplane in Vermont

for Red and Eleanor Warren

He watched a cloud. It brought him
the shape of one horse or another:
"Was it Cinders? I disremember . . .
a big trot . . . early autumn,
grass to the pommel. September."

Toward dark the ridges smothered
day. The rattling wagon
winnowed birds. How smart
his bays—"like hens on hot stone"—
that drew us along. I've discovered

the painter's failure of heart.
I've tried to draw his face
from the land, his language, the land
in his language: "Damn the wind!
Enough to shake owls from the trees!"

They come back, every phrase;
but I've lost his face in the clouds.
You learn in time to fail.
He spat on the hardening road,
bad heel propped on the rail,

as out of the grainfields the geese
flew, the time flew, September
he darkened and died.

Heart rattles. Strange as disease
or god, the airplane roars

down the ridges. Wind shakes. Auroras
rise and whack at the sky.
Frost on the tarmac glints
and goes out like sparks off hooves,
or the face I can't remember,

but off to the west I squint
at a spot out of actual sight,
and Billy mounts and moves.

Band Concert

for Kate Emlen and Robin Barone

The bus, like a dozing monster,
nods yellow in high summer's grass
by the monument. We read its legend:
McCutcheon's Student Band.

All unchanged, they do the standards:
"Semper Fidelis," "A Grand Old Flag,"
assorted Sousas. The saxes crack
a note behind. McCutcheon beams.

The grocer dances to "Don't Fence Me In"
with a farmer's daughter. Two grim
Mormons stray among the pickup trucks,
dark volumes in their hands;

townsmen palm their beers and blush
their choked-down laughter.
Now the marching: vague hints of footwork.
And what if one day we do go under?

The kids whirl, frantic, on the seeding green.
The same plump blonde dips her baton
in kerosene. The finale flames
when she sparks her lighter.

The distant ocean blows thickly in-
to night that lies down soft on the crowd.

Moths and car horns swim the air.
July the Fourth, and more than ever

the old folks stiffen to "The Star-Spangled Banner."
Then everyone sings, "Let the Rest of the World
Go By." And rapt, at the edge of things,
McCutcheon glows in a flick of thunder.

Drooge's Barn

for Robert Pack

Look if you like
through the roof beams;
but don't compare them to ribs.

Knock at the empty troughs.
You will not get a ghost's halloo
nor, failing, find your subject

in the silence. Stones in the cellar,
boards on the floor, are stones and boards,
not crying, not refusing to cry.

Yet of course you insist
on listening. And what you hear is a hound,
ragging the same white hare by moon

that he ragged all day by day.
His voice is a chop—like a hound's voice,
not an ax, a hoe, an adz.

Through the adz-smoothed beams
you find the familiar moon.
If it throws hieroglyphs on the walls,

it does so according to laws.
Underfoot, the chicken dust is hard
as slate, your breath is a vertical string

on nights like this so clear
you are aching to call them uncanny.
But the barn sags according to laws—

climate, time, and taxes.
Make no room for magic,
make no room for despair.

The dog's tune doubles and redoubles,
the punk in the floorboards glows, the moon
divides, beam after beam.

For Don C., against a Proverb

"The simple are killed by their turning away."

I use examples:
you blew away

an insect's froth
to find him hidden

as in a pew.
I've seen you kneel

to sniff a stone
or chafe a bone,

bringing the full-fleshed,
fly-strafed, stamping

beast to mind.
Once, bent beachward

at the lake, you tried
to name the maker

of some human track,
imagine his mission,

his conversation.
Don, for you

I'm flouting Scripture.
Spiders sew

the woods together.
Limb to limb.

The sun assumes
one color, then

another, others.
Likewise moon

and dust and dew.
Your sermon was weather,

things, stars:
now *they* could write

their meanings, and none
was a dream of some

dim future. Home
for you was always

salt-scent that rose
from working clothes,

the snap and hiss
in a stewpot, blood

and down on wife
and sons amid

the frantic dance
of slaughtered chickens,

agony
about the ribs

where love laid on
a velvet whip.

I've thought of the death,
of how some death

like yours should make
the Proverbs blanch

in shame. I bring
to mind the hand,

hard-horned and bursting
pods to see

familiar seeds
take wind. They rise

at dawn against
the whitening sky

like those last hardy
melancholy

stars afloat
in bright new morning—

stars that won't
put themselves out,

nor quite turn out
till they are blown out.

Revision of the Seasons

i

On a slickened limb the saw-whet grates
his scritch of winter and unease.
Blank night. The house gathers
to shudder in spite of you,
your wife with her taut womb,
your fire-warmed dogs,
all the celebrations down on paper.

The pony knocks his stall and the stars
hide out. The thaw was an old illusion,
the splendid geese of spring are lost,
and the snow—you hear it stiffen.

Old poems are falling.

You work against the grimace: birth,
howl of a dog in the cold, tin kick
of a pony, small owl's threat.

Robed and strange, you pace,
changing the words,
around and around,
in the empty halls.

ii

Spring comes.
The doors hang plumb
again; there is no

challenge like no challenge,
no thing so blank
as plain sufficiency: the mist
each day unfolding into sun,
the clarity you wanted
and you want undone.

iii

June to August a happy torpor
you recall as pain.

iv

In the woods, the hares are turning white
as pages. Flickers gather, shocking white
in bursts along the hardening lanes,
the hedgerows. Dark late roses tint
the water in a kitchen glass.
You cannot tell what you're revising.

Elegy at Peter Dana Point

Elegy at Peter Dana Point

for Creston MacArthur (1917–76)

Strips of shingle and bright can torn
from shack roofs, salt and sand, and saw-
dust from the housing project, fly in a wind
that drives the lake in a wild winter thaw.
A single high-top sneaker wheels
crazy on its lace, slip-knotted to a limb.
Dogs hunker, cringe, and moan
against the north wall of a shed of tin,
where half untacked a poster peels
itself away: "Keep Maine's Forests Green."

The Indian point: the men in clean
white shirts, bought in town at the clean-out sale,
and mostly down on luck. Old Lola still gets on,
though his one good eye is pale
as powdered mustard. His oldest son,
the home-run hitter, rolls on the foot
shot up in Vietnam. They never did
find that ball he hit
in the Topsfield game, the one
the boys took in the bottom

of the ninth. What in Christ's gotten
into the weather? The power's failed
from here to the coast. No radio, no forecast.
And the oldest woman out here can't think
of such a day, so early. In bed
at home, she nurses the hurt in her black last
tooth: she fetches a drink

against it—hot liquor for her failed
old jaws and her hands, all gnurled and red
by the stove. The crack

of weather jitters her. All this wreck—
high water and wind and loss of power—
settles down on this hour.
She calls it a sign, and so do we,
less certain what we mean. Snowdrops hiss
against the windows. A churchyard tree is down,
branches snapped like savaged flowers.
What elegy in the face of this?
Perhaps we'll remember your own bold song,
to the music of an old-time sawyers' band:

"St. Regis thinks it owns the land
Where we hunt the ducks and geese;
St. Regis must be getting poor,
They want a dollar's lease.
We'll see they never get that fee,
For we've got things well in hand;
And St. Regis may be told some day
The MacArthurs own the land."
I remember one fall a single loon, calling for open water.

Today, another loon sculls in midwinter
on Long Lake. A raven pumps and swerves
overhead, fighting a blast of sky.
Red workmen in khaki lift steel hats
as you roll by.
Fox tracks,
deer tracks

pick through the graves.
In the brush, the rusted head of an ax.
All your mourners know what they're weeping for

in the gaps of this mud-and-thunder roar;
but a few stand out, like beaver huts:
Lola and Leo, and old Earl, grim
as always, who called you "Gus";
and straight as a string your Uncle Jim,
with his strawberry nose, and full of rye;
"Three-Dollar" Bill, who blinks his eyes
like an owl; and down from Milltown, half-breed Dave,
the one you called "The Blue-Eyed Brave,"
who called you "Warden's Nightmare."

Something has changed in the air.
You almost smell spring, but not as it was,
now with the speedboats, the long-log saws,
electric fish-finders, and the company!
Sponging a buck to lie on the ground!
We'd have seen they never got that fee,
made sure they never found
the two of us, back far enough to scare them to death
in that corner near Thousand-Acre Heath
with its early trout, where we saw the skulls

with antlers locked, in that slough so full
of trillium. Lovely, but how they reeked!
Like hell itself. Now Lola throws
a rose in the hole, and Earl a choke-
cherry sprig. Jim's drunken bunch blows
away, into cedar and oak.

And I, what posy do I have to leave?
A knot of grief,
the flowered turn of my eulogy:

"He loved life. He loved children. Good company.
Good times. From him, let us learn
that the sharing of pleasures is sacred to God."
(Yet I mean the smokes, rolled neat to burn
smooth and cool; that light on the ridge we never
    understood;
the first flight of woodcock; the last swarm of gnats;
the driftless calm on Flipper Creek,
when the geese eased by us, coasting the slick,
and we watched them, still as wildcats,
the near-purple sheen of their heads.)

The wind is suddenly dead,
its absence deep as was its rage.
The sun winds through the trees
and a white jay settles to gawk from the gate;
the minds of the mourners, of your age
or better, will rise
to Slewgundy, Pocumcus, Jones's Mistake
in the lull—for a moment, our small spites die.
The loon, alone, is fighting to fly
clear of its wake. We return

to our lives, away from The Burn,
from Bear Trap Landing, Jemison's Fate,
Unknown Stream, The Overnight Hole,
Dark Cove Mountain, Three-Dawn Lake—
but old names blow through us like consecration.

Old names, old places, bring back you:
you knew them, touched them, boot, paddle, and pole.
Our elegy is your invention,
because you touched us, as seasons do.

Poetry from Illinois